MW00650576

LET'S EXPLORE AUSTRIA
(MOST FAMOUS ATTRACTIONS IN AUSTRIA)

BABY PROFESSOR
EDUCATION KIDS

Speedy Publishing LLC
40 E. Main St. #1156
Newark, DE 19711
www.speedypublishing.com

Copyright 2018

All Rights reserved. No part of this book may be reproduced or used in any way or form or by any means whether electronic or mechanical, this means that you cannot record or photocopy any material ideas or tips that are provided in this book.

Austria, one of Europe's most popular holiday destinations, attracts tourists year-round.

Schönbrunn Palace is one of the most important architectural, cultural and historical monuments in the country.

Hallstatt is a village in the Salzkammergut, a region in Austria. Hallstatt is known for its production of salt.

Hofburg Palace is the former imperial palace in the centre of Vienna. Hofburg Palace was for centuries the seat of Austria's monarchy, the powerful Habsburgs.

The Krimml Waterfalls are the highest waterfall in Austria. Krimmler Waterfalls is a tiered waterfall. The waterfall begins at the top of the Krimmler Ache valley, and plunges downward in three stages.

The Eisriesenwelt is a natural limestone ice cave located in Werfen, Austria. It is the largest ice cave in the world.

The Grossglockner High Alpine Road is the highest surfaced mountain pass road in Austria. The road is named after the Grossglockner, Austria's highest mountain.

The Vienna State Opera is an opera house. It is located in the centre of Vienna, Austria. The orchestra is recognized as one of the top in the world.

CPSIA information can be obtained
at www.ICGtesting.com
Printed in the USA
LVHW050717070622
720660LV00007B/386

9 781682 609385